ART PROFILES
For Kids

LEONARDO DA VINCI

P.O. Box 196
Hockessin, Delaware 19707
Visit us on the web: www.mitchelllane.com
Comments? email us: mitchelllane@mitchelllane.com

ART PROFILES FOR KIDS

Titles in the Series

Art Profiles For Kids

LEONARDO DA VINCI

Kathleen Tracy

Mitchell Lane PUBLISHERS

P.O. Box 196
Hockessin, Delaware 19707
Visit us on the web: www.mitchelllane.com
Comments? email us: mitchelllane@mitchelllane.com

Printing   1   2   3   4   5   6   7   8   9

Library of Congress Cataloging-in-Publication Data
Tracy, Kathleen.
  Leonardo da Vinci / by Kathleen Tracy.
      p. cm. — (Art profiles for kids)
  Includes bibliographical references and index.
  ISBN 978-1-58415-711-3 (library bound)
  I. Leonardo, da Vinci, 1452–1519—Juvenile literature. 2. Artists—Italy—Biography—Juvenile literature. 3. Scientists—Italy—Biography—Juvenile literature. I. Leonardo, da Vinci, 1452–1519. II. Title.
  N6923.L33T73 2009
  709.2—dc22
  [B]
                                                                2008020938

ABOUT THE AUTHOR: Kathleen Tracy has been a journalist for over twenty years. Her writing has been featured in magazines including *The Toronto Star*'s "Star Week," *A&E Biography* magazine, *KidScreen* and *TV Times*. She is also the author of numerous books for Mitchell Lane Publishers including *William Hewlett: Pioneer of the Computer Age*, *The Fall of the Berlin Wall*, *Paul Cézanne*, *The Story of September 11, 2001*, *Johnny Depp*, *Mariah Carey*, and *Kelly Clarkson*.

ABOUT THE COVER: The images on the cover are paintings by the various artists in this series.

PLB

Art Profiles for Kids

There are two versions of Leonardo's *Virgin of the Rocks*. Art historians believe the version on display at the National Gallery in London, above, was completed mostly by Leonardo's assistant Ambrogio de Predis. The version at the Louvre in Paris is believed to have been painted primarily by Leonardo.

Legal Woes

The Catholic monks in Milan were beside themselves. Leonardo da Vinci had come highly recommended. He was known as one of the most gifted, inventive artists of the day. He had seemed the perfect choice for painting a piece for San Francesco Grande's chapel of the Immaculate Conception. And Leonardo had readily agreed to the contract offered by the monks. The contract called for the painting, intended to be the chapel's altarpiece, to be delivered in eight months. But the deadline had passed and Leonardo had yet to finish the painting he named *The Virgin of the Rocks*. The monks waited patiently, but as month after month passed, they grew increasingly frustrated. Finally, at wit's end, they resorted to drastic measures and sued Leonardo for not fulfilling the terms of his contract.

When the monks had approached Leonardo about the commission in 1483, it was a great coup for the artist. *The Virgin of the Rocks* (also known as *The Madonna of the Rocks*) was one of his first commissions in Milan. Having it prominently displayed in a major church would no doubt bring more commissions and further Leonardo's reputation and status. The contract for the painting was very specific. *The Virgin of the Rocks* was to signify the Immaculate Conception, a Catholic dogma that says Mary conceived Jesus without original sin. The Virgin Mary was to be the focus of the painting. Da Vinci was to portray her in a pure, holy manner, and she should have angels surrounding her. The monks even detailed what colors the characters' clothes should be, and that the background be a combination of mountains and rocks. It all sounded simple enough; it turned out to be anything but.

Leonardo asked his assistant, Ambrogio de Predis, to work on the painting with him. Initially, everything seemed to be proceeding smoothly. The painting was due before the annual Feast of the Immaculate Conception, celebrated on December 8. Even under perfect conditions, Leonardo was not the most punctual of artists. While he would become known as one of the greatest Renaissance artists, he was also one of the least prolific. Perhaps because he was so inquisitive about everything around him, he suffered from a habitually short attention span and found it difficult to finish an art project before turning his attention elsewhere. His unfinished works greatly outnumber his finished canvases.

In addition to Leonardo's chronic tardiness, a financial dispute arose over *The Virgin of the Rocks*. Although Leonardo had been paid in full by the monks when he signed the contract, he and Ambrogio asked for an additional payment to cover their out-of-pocket expenses—the gold-leaf frame Leonardo chose, plus the cost of having it carved, used a big chunk of his commission.

The monks rejected Leonardo's first version of the *Virgin* and sued. Leonardo retained ownership of the painting and eventually gave it to French King Louis XII. The legal dispute remained deadlocked in the courts for years. Finally, in 1506, aided by the intervention of Louis XII, the lawsuit was resolved. Afterward the monks commissioned Leonardo for a second *Virgin*. This time, the contract gave him and Ambrogio two years to complete the work. They were paid just half of what they earned for the first painting.

By this time, some Milan officials were fed up with Leonardo's now infamous procrastination. One wrote that Leonardo "has not borne himself as he ought to have done towards this republic, in that he has received a good sum of money and has made little beginning of a great work which he is under obligation to execute, and has already comported himself as a laggard . . ."[1] However, Leonardo managed to meet the deadline, and the second *Virgin of the Rocks* was finally hung in the chapel on August 18, 1508—twenty-five years late.

It is believed that Leonardo was the sole artist on the first *Virgin of the Rocks,* because the painting shows his unique workmanship; specifically his use of chiaroscuro, which is the use of light and dark to create an illusion of depth. The changes in tone are very subtle, an example of sfumato, a painting technique in which the artist uses translucent layers of color to create perceptions of depth and to blend colors so that there is no perceptible transition from one color to the next. Leonardo also added a personal touch by turning one of the designated angels into St. John.

It is also believed that Ambrogio painted the angels that appear on panels on either side of the painting. According to author Kenneth Clark, "One of these survives and is in the National Gallery [of London] beside the second version of the *Virgin of the Rocks.* . . . The other was evidently moved when the first version of Leonardo's picture was taken to France, and a substitute by one of Leonardo's pupils put in its place. This angel is lost and the substitute now hangs in the National Gallery, where it long passed as the work of Predis, although technically it has nothing in common with the Predis angel opposite to it."[2]

The second version of the painting uses brighter colors and more blue tones. St. John is now holding a cross and Leonardo added haloes over the Virgin Mary, St. John, and Jesus. Many experts believe that Leonardo probably only supervised the second version and left the actual painting to other artists in his studio. The second *Virgin* remained in the chapel until 1781. For many years the painting passed through the hands of private collectors until it eventually found a permanent home in London's National Gallery.

Ambrogio de Predis, who had previously established himself as an illuminator, continued working as a portrait painter, frequently working with royalty, such as Ludovico Sforza, the Duke of Milan. In 1493 he went to Innsbruck and stayed with the new wife of Emperor Maximilian I, who was Sforza's daughter. He supplemented his art earnings by designing stage sets, coins, and tapestries. The highlight of his career would be working with Leonardo on *Virgin of the Rocks,* and only two known Predis portraits survive.

The prolonged legal wrangling had no effect on Leonardo's reputation—or his propensity for tardiness. In 1495, while he was still in Milan—with the *Virgin of the Rocks* litigation still ongoing—Leonardo was commissioned to paint a fresco of a Passover dinner in the dining hall at Santa Maria della Grazie. A fresco is a technique used on walls and ceilings where the artist applies a layer of plaster, then paints on it using watercolors. The drawbacks are that the artist must finish before the plaster dries, and because of this time factor, the color range for the paints is limited. Not surprisingly, Leonardo was unable to work fast enough when using plaster, so he developed his own method of applying plaster that would give him the ability to change the fresco at a later date.

Leonardo's work habits drove the Santa Maria monks crazy. He would work one day for eighteen hours, then disappear for the rest of the week. He might sit and study the work-in-progress for hours, then, after adding one or two minor brushstrokes, leave and be gone for days again. Weeks turned into months, which turned into years. When the head of the monastery, the prior, complained, Leonardo shrugged it off. Three years later, in 1498, the fresco was finally complete.

In the painting, which depicts Jesus and his final meal with his disciples, Leonardo used the same type of table linens and place settings that the monks used, which gave the impression that Jesus and the Apostles were dining alongside the monks. Unfortunately, though, the experimental method Leonardo used to prepare the wall was flawed, and within just a few years, flakes of pigment had begun to peel. Even damaged, *The Last Supper* would become one of Leonardo's most famous works. It would also be the source of a controversy—and a mystery—that would rage well into the twenty-first century.

The Renaissance

The Renaissance refers to a cultural movement that brought Europe out of the Dark Ages and into a period marked by intellectual and artistic advances. Although there is disagreement as to when exactly the Renaissance began, it is generally considered to have spanned from the late Middle Ages of the fifteenth century through the seventeenth century. The era got its name because certain classical ideas were reborn—or experienced a renaissance ("rebirth")—when long-forgotten ancient writings were rediscovered by the scholars of the day.

Although the Renaissance had a profound impact on European culture in general, affecting politics, religion, philosophy, science, and literature, it is probably best known as a time of great achievements in painting and sculpture. Hallmarks of Renaissance paintings include religious themes, the use of realism, and the depiction of human emotion. Later, this style would be known as *classical* art.

The consensus among historians is that the Renaissance began in Florence, Italy. At the time, Florence was a thriving center of the arts, in part because wealthy families such as the Medici offered patronage to artists such as Leonardo da Vinci, Botticelli, and Michelangelo. From Florence, the movement quickly spread to the rest of Italy and then throughout Europe. The invention of the printing press allowed ideas to be spread faster than ever before, and each region incorporated those ideas uniquely into its culture.

Boticelli's Self-Portrait

Over the several hundred years since then, historians' opinions about the Renaissance have changed. In the nineteenth century, the advances of thought and art during the Renaissance were seen as a distinct break from medieval attitudes; overall it was seen as a much more enlightened time, when new ideas were more readily accepted and put into practice. In more recent times, however, the Renaissance has been viewed as a more natural cultural progression from medieval times, and the eras' similarities, rather than the differences, are emphasized.

Andrea del Verrocchio was an influential fifteenth-century artist who mentored many young artists, including Leonardo and Botticelli. Leonardo assisted him on *The Baptism of Christ* (above), painting the blond angel on the left and the background. Some historians credit Botticelli with painting the second angel. The painting is displayed at the Uffizi Gallery in Florence, Italy.

Prodigy

In the center of Italy is a picturesque region called Tuscany, known for its beautiful countryside, its artistic history, and its capital, Florence. Fifty miles from Florence is the town of Vinci. A one-time fortress, it was founded around 1250 and was where Leonardo grew up. He was born at 10:30 in the evening on April 15, 1452, in Anchiano, a village near Vinci. Leonardo's father, Ser Piero, an up-and-coming notary, never married Leonardo's mother, a peasant named Caterina, because she was socially beneath him.

Leonardo lived with his mother until she married, then spent time with his paternal grandparents. By 1457 he was living with Ser Piero, whose wife was unable to have children. His father was emotionally distant and strict, but his wife, Donna Albiera, doted on Leonardo.

While Ser Piero may not have been emotionally nurturing, he gave his son the best education available to an illegitimate child. Leonardo was a gifted student, showing an intense curiosity in the world around him. One of his earliest memories—which may have been real or may have been a dream—was from when he was a toddler. A hawk landed on him and stuck its tail feathers in the boy's mouth. The experience was imprinted into Leonardo's brain, and from that point on he was fascinated, to the point of obsession, with flight.

For all his academic prowess, the circumstances of Leonardo's birth would limit his career options. Among the aristocratic class, being born out of wedlock was not a big deal. Illegitimate sons were still allowed to inherit their father's property and money. But among the middle class, being born without a legal father carried a stigma, or deep social disapproval. While Ser Piero was very successful, he was still middle class. All the clubs, guilds, and unions that would have been freely available to Leonardo had his parents been married when he was born would now scrutinize him. Also, he would not be able to enroll in a university or even be a notary like his father. Despite his obvious intelligence and talents, Leonardo's future was poised to be unorthodox.

One of Leonardo's closest family relationships was with his paternal uncle Francesco, who ran a farm. While visiting his uncle, Leonardo helped tend the animals. He also spent hours exploring and just observing nature—the same landscapes that he would later sketch and study.

Because Leonardo was not expected to follow in his father's professional footsteps, he could pursue his own interests, such as drawing. He took an almost perverse pride in the fact that he couldn't attend college and therefore was never formally educated in subjects such as physics or Latin.

Dr. Sherwin Nuland from the Yale School of Medicine noted, "He used to call himself an unlettered man, and he pointed out that the only way to really learn things was to learn them on one's own and not from the work of the ancients. He was fond of writing, for example, in his notebooks that certainly one can drink from bottles where water has been stored, but isn't it better to drink directly from the spring, which is what he did. And he felt always that his very poor Latin and even worse Greek was a great advantage to him because it essentially forced him to do experimentations on his own, make observations on his own, make correlations on his own."[1]

Leonardo's unique creative eye and his interest in science were evident at a young age. According to a frequently told story, Ser Piero once asked his son to paint a round shield. Leonardo decided he wanted the shield to have a monster on it, so he went outside and collected a variety of specimens such as lizards and bats and even maggots, using the creepy features of nature for his artistic inspiration. He was so focused on painting his monster that Leonardo didn't notice how his specimens were decomposing—and beginning to smell. When Ser Piero saw the finished shield, he knew Leonardo had a special gift.

"He grew up into a youth of shining promise, gifted in many directions," wrote biographer Irma Anne Richter. "Besides developing his own style of drawing, he modeled heads of smiling women and children in clay which showed the hands of a master. He studied music and was resolved to acquire the art of playing the lyre."[2]

When Leonardo was still a teenager, his father arranged to have him apprenticed as a *garzone,* or studio boy, to a well-known Florentine artist and sculptor named Andrea del Verrocchio. In the fifteenth century, being an artist was a respected career and one Leonardo could pursue freely. He joined other students at Verrocchio's studios, where they learned to make brushes, mix colors, sculpt in bronze and marble, and paint. At that time, when an artist received a commission to create a painting, it was understood that his apprentices would assist in the work. It didn't take long for Verrocchio to recognize Leonardo's talent, and he used him in his most important project, *The Baptism of Christ.*

In 1472, when Leonardo was twenty, he was accepted into the painter's guild. He quickly earned a reputation for his skill and creativity. But even then he was known for seldom finishing projects he started. While Leonardo enjoyed the challenge presented by painting—planning it, developing the idea, determining the palette—the painstaking work of actually applying the paint interested him much less. Plus, when he was inside painting, he wasn't outside pursuing his other passion: observing nature.

Leonardo was still in his twenties when he began keeping detailed notebooks that included scientific observations, personal commentary, ideas for inventions, sketches, and mechanical drawings. He found science endlessly intriguing and was particularly interested in anatomy. To learn about the inner workings of people and animals, he would dissect corpses and animal carcasses to study the muscles and bones. He drew detailed pictures of plants and rocks, and recorded their unique features.

Leonardo began keeping detailed notebooks when he was in his twenties. He would write down observations about nature, draw sketches and also use the notebooks as a person journal. His first known sketch is *Study of a Tuscan Landscape,* dated 1473.

He would use this deep understanding of the natural world in his paintings. Leonardo was unique in another way: He was left-handed. At that time, many people associated left-handedness with evil, so left-handed children were usually forced to write right-handed. But Leonardo was a proud southpaw and never switched. Some have suggested that his unique way of seeing the world was connected to his left-handedness.

According to descriptions of him, Leonardo was also strikingly handsome—graceful, strong, and charming. It seemed as if he was on the fast track to success. Then an unexpected scandal threatened to derail his career—and his freedom.

Andrea del Verrocchio

Verrocchio was born Andrea di Michele di Francesco de' Cioni in Florence in 1435. His father, Michele de' Cioni, worked as a tile maker and in later years, a tax collector. Michele never married, so when Andrea began apprenticing as a goldsmith with Giulio Verrocchio, he took his mentor's last name. Initially, Andrea found success in a variety of fields, from jewelry making to sculpture, working with a wide range of materials, including marble, terra-cotta, silver, and bronze. His most noted sculpture was the bronze group *Christ and Doubting of Thomas*, or *Christ and St. Thomas*.

Christ and St. Thomas

It is believed he started painting sometime in the 1460s. By 1475, Verrocchio's art studio had become a training ground for many young artists such as Lorenzo di Credi, Luca Signorelli, and Leonardo. The paintings created at Verrocchio's studio were mostly collaborations, with assistance from his students. Leonardo assisted on Verrocchio's *The Baptism of Christ*, which is considered by art historians as one of the best examples of Early Renaissance Florentine art. Leonardo's skill was apparent. Legend has it that after it became clear that the pupil had surpassed his teacher, Verrocchio swore never to paint again. While no doubt apocryphal, the story highlights Leonardo's innate talent.

By the late 1470s, Verrocchio devoted his time to sculpture. Like his contemporaries Michelangelo and Donatello, Verrocchio also sculpted a statue of David, although Verrocchio's work shows the hero as a youth. In 1478 the Republic of Venice commissioned Verrocchio to create an equestrian statue to honor the Venetian army commander Colleoni. In his will, Colleoni had left the Republic of Venice a large sum of money to pay for the monument. The piece Verrocchio designed was unique because it was the first attempt to sculpt a horse with all four legs off the ground. Verrocchio submitted a wax model in 1480 and moved to Venice in 1488 to prepare the sculpture's cast. He died later that year, before the work was finished.

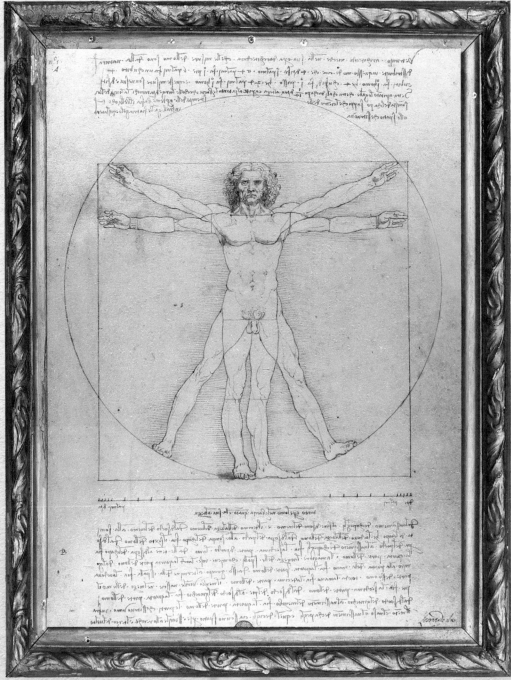

Leonardo had a deep interest in human anatomy and the proportions found in nature. He was influenced by the Roman architect Marcus Vitruvius, who postulated that if a compass were centered at a person's navel, their fingers and toes would touch the circumference of the drawn circle; likewise, the distance from the feet to the head is the same as the length of a person's outstretched arms, making a square. Leonardo illustrated Vitruvius' belief in the drawing *The Vitruvian Man*, c. 1485.

The Artist

Leonardo was twenty-four years old and still working as Verrocchio's apprentice when he became embroiled in a controversy that could have ended his career as an artist. In 1476 he and three other young men were charged with sodomy, or having a physical relationship with another man. According to court documents, Leonardo was accused of a sexual relationship with Jacopo Saltarelli, a seventeen-year-old who modeled in Verrocchio's studio and who also worked as a prostitute.

At that time, although homosexuality was common in the Florentine artists' community, being formally convicted of sodomy was extremely serious. In 1432, Florence became the first city in Europe to set up a special department, called the *Ufficiali di Notte* (Officers of the Night), whose sole purpose was to find and arrest homosexuals. If convicted, Leonardo would have been prevented from working on commission for the Church, a significant source of income for Renaissance artists. He would also be subject to punishment by the Vatican, the government of the Catholic Church. The punishments ranged from a public confession to more serious sentences such as banishment, imprisonment, or execution. At the time the pope was Sixtus IV, who would later approve the Spanish Inquisition, so a guilty verdict would be ominous.

The charges against Leonardo were based on an anonymous tip. Although accusing someone of having a homosexual relationship was a common tactic to cause trouble for an enemy, most historians agree that Leonardo was romantically attracted to men, not women. Throughout his

life, his closest relationships were with young men. He frequently sketched pictures of males depicting frontal nudity, but he rarely drew pictures of women from the neck down, and the few he did portray were not very accurate in terms of female anatomy. There is also no evidence that he ever had a physical relationship with a woman, or even a close friendship.

While it may not have been surprising that Leonardo was homosexual, the bigger mystery is who would want to make an accusation that could ruin the young artist. Authorities kept Leonardo in custody for two months. The case came before the courts twice, but on both occasions the charges were dropped for lack of evidence.

After his release, there is no record of Leonardo's work or even his whereabouts for two years (he resurfaces in historical documents in 1478). The trauma of the accusation seems to have had a profound impact on Leonardo. He became obsessively private about his personal life, even using "mirror writing" to prevent others from reading his written thoughts. Considering that the *Ufficiali di Notte* kept Leonardo under surveillance for some time after the trial, he had a reason to be paranoid. Because of his secrecy, however, a large portion of his life was lost to history.

Writer Miranda Seymour notes, "The problem with Leonardo is that we know so little about him. . . . Living in the city of one of Italy's greatest art patrons, Lorenzo de' Medici, Leonardo seems never to have found favor at court. All that is known . . . is that he fancied himself, wearing daringly short tunics and a long, carefully maintained beard and that his interest in beautiful young men who may have been lovers, adopted sons, or both, is well documented."[1]

While his personal life may have been enigmatic, Leonardo's painting was very much in the public eye. Although through the course of his career he produced a relatively small number of canvases, his revolutionary use of colors and unique style made him one of the most influential artists of the Renaissance.

The first painting Leonardo completed entirely by himself was the *Madonna and the Child*—in 1478, the same year he became an independent master. Another composition from that time is of a young boy eating

In 1478 Leonardo painted *Madonna and the Child* (right), also known as the *Benois Madonna*, after artist Leon Benois who came into possession of it.

Leonardo's first painting of the Madonna was the *Madonna with a Pomegranate*, although there are some who argue the primary artist was Verrocchio.

The Litta Madonna was named for the Litta family, who owned it for hundreds of years until Alexander II of Russia acquired it.

sherbet, and a portrait of Ginevra de' Benci. Between 1480 and 1481, he created a small Annunciation painting, which now hangs in the Louvre. He left an equal number of projects unfinished, including his first commission, which was to paint an altarpiece for the chapel of the Palazzo Vecchio, the Florentine town hall. Also unfinished were a work of St. Jerome and a painting called *The Adoration of the Magi* for the Monastery of San Donato a Scopeto. Leonardo spent considerable time planning the painting, and he produced extensive drawings. The painting itself incorporates a new composition technique by grouping primary figures in the foreground, with the background depicting vague images of ruins and battle scenes, giving the work atmospheric perspective.

Before the *Adoration of the Magi* was finished, Leonardo accepted a commission by Ludovico Sforza, the Duke of Milan. In 1482 he made Milan

Adoration of the Magi measures eight feet by nine feet. It is believed that the shepherd boy standing to the far right, in the foreground, is a self-portrait of Leonardo as a young boy. Although the painting was unfinished, which is why it is only in shades of brown, more sketches have been found of this work than any of Leonardo's other paintings.

his home and stayed for the next seventeen years. During that time, Leonardo was at the height of his artistic creativity.

Working for the duke was a full-time commitment, keeping Leonardo busy painting, sculpting, and designing lavish court festivals. His studio provided his apprentices and students with a vibrant, creative atmosphere. The duke also utilized Leonardo's scientific insight and had him designing machinery, weapons, and buildings, including churches and forts. Between 1485 and 1490, Leonardo produced studies of nature, flying machines, mathematics, canals, and architecture. It was also during this period that Leonardo produced his first anatomical studies, including *The Vitruvian Man*, named after the Roman author and architect Vitruvius. Vitruvius designed buildings based on the proportions of the human body. He believed if a perfectly proportioned human extended his arms and legs, they would fit perfectly in both a circle and a square. Da Vinci's illustration—a man in a circle combined with a man in a square—vividly explains this principle.

Because da Vinci devoted so much time to his scientific endeavors, he finished only six paintings, but they are among the world's most famous. One of his first commissions in Milan was *The Last Supper*, which was to be painted in Santa Maria delle Grazi. The fresco is renowned for its clever composition and use of perspective. The Apostles are grouped in threes and frame Jesus, located in the center of the painting. Leonardo's use of shadow was also unprecedented.

Even though the painting had seriously deteriorated within fifty years of its completion, it continued to influence other artists profoundly. It is considered so important a work that beginning in 1726, numerous efforts and considerable money has been spent trying to restore it—all of them largely unsuccessful. Modern technology, however, has reversed some of the damage and is at least preventing further deterioration.

One of Leonardo's most challenging commissions was a sculpture of the duke's father riding a horse. Initially the bronze statue was only supposed to be life-sized. Later the duke decided that the homage to his father should be larger than life. Twenty-four feet high and weighing nearly

80 tons, the sculpture pushed Leonardo to his creative limits. He spent years designing the sculpture by studying and sketching the movement of horses and developing new casting techniques to accommodate the size of the statue. He had gotten as far as making a twenty-two-foot clay model but abandoned the project after the French invaded Milan and removed the duke from power in 1499. The model did not survive—French archers destroyed it by using it for target practice.

Leonardo returned to Florence in 1500, and a year later began working on an altarpiece titled *The Virgin and Child with Saint Anne*. Yet again he left the painting unfinished when he accepted another commission. In 1502, Cesare Borgia hired him as a military engineer. Borgia was the son of Pope Alexander VI. He was expected to follow his father into the clergy, but instead pursued a military career and earned a reputation as being ruthless and ambitious. Leonardo found Borgia's tactics offensive and eventually quit.

Back in Florence, Leonardo worked on three of his last major paintings. The first, which became his most celebrated, was the *Mona Lisa*, also known as *La Gioconda*, or *Portrait of Lisa Gherardini, Wife of Francesco del Giocondo*. Leonardo was so attached to the painting, he actually traveled with it. While the *Mona Lisa*'s enigmatic smile has intrigued people for centuries, it was Leonardo's use of the innovative techniques sfumato and chiaroscuro—of which he was one of the first great masters—that makes the painting so arresting.

Although the painting is supposed to be a portrait of a merchant's wife, it has been the subject of endless speculation. Some experts suggest it is actually an idealized image of Leonardo's mother; others argue it is a self-portrait. Nobody really knows, and it is that air of mystery that has helped make the *Mona Lisa* arguably the most famous painting in history.

Another painting that has generated considerable discussion among art historians is *Leda and the Swan*, which shows the rape of Leda by Zeus, who takes the form of a swan to trick her. It is the only painting in Leonardo's body of work that features a female nude. It is also one of his only pictures inspired by classical mythology. His vision of the myth of

Leonardo's *The Virgin and Child with Saint Anne.* Yet another unfinished work, it is believed Leonardo finished the background, St. Anne, the Virgin, and the Child before he lost interest and turned to another project. The lamb is believed to have been finished by another artist, and the drapery over the Virgin's legs is barely more than an outline.

Zeus and Leda reflects his scientific sensibilities that anything out of the natural order borders on the grotesque.

In his later years, Leonardo was sought after as an art consultant. In 1503 he was appointed to an artists' panel whose task was to select a location for Michelangelo's marble statue of David (now housed in Florence's *Accademia* gallery). That same year, Leonardo began designing a wall painting of the battle of Anghiari, intended for the Palazzo Vecchio's great hall. The battle had been an important victory for Florence in its recent war with Pisa. Again, Leonardo got as far as a detailed first sketch in 1505, but never completed the painting. Whatever was finished was probably destroyed in the seventeenth century. Several copies made by other artists still survive, including one by Peter Paul Rubens that hangs in the Louvre.

In 2000, however, art investigator Maurizio Seracini announced that he believed he had found the lost picture. "Experts who have been searching for years for a fresco painted by Leonardo da Vinci in the Palazzo Vecchio in Florence are convinced they have located it at last," reported *The Daily Telegraph*. "They believe that the *Battle of Anghiari* lies hidden beneath another fresco, by Giorgio Vasari."[2]

Seracini was hoping to determine what, if anything, lay beneath Vasari's fresco by using a hi-tech neutron X-ray to see beneath the top layers of paint. The discovery would be of immense importance because there are only seventeen known completed paintings by Leonardo da Vinci.

On July 9, 1504, Leonardo received news that his father had died. Even though Ser Piero had openly acknowledged Leonardo as his son, his seventeen half-siblings conspired to cut Leonardo out of any inheritance. When his adored uncle died, however, Leonardo was better prepared and prevented his half-siblings from again cutting him out. After some wrangling, he received a financial settlement and the use of his uncle's land. Although he was not rich, he was comfortable enough that he did not have to take every art commission offered him. What the art world would lose, the scientific world would gain.

Inquisition

An Inquisition is a tribunal, or court, appointed by the Catholic Church. These courts were used to find and punish heresy, which is any action that opposes the teaching of Catholicism. The first Inquisition was established by Pope Lucius III in the twelfth century. In 1233, Pope Gregory IX instituted an Inquisition to combat a heretical sect in France. By 1255, the purge of heretics had spread throughout much of Western Europe. In 1478, Pope Sixtus IV approved an Inquisition arranged by Spain's King Ferdinand and Queen Isabella.

Unlike earlier Inquisitions, the one in Spain was run independently of the Vatican and was overseen by the monarchy. Its primary goal was to target Jewish and Islamic converts who were suspected of secretly practicing their old religions—a good possibility, since many had been forced to convert. Later, Protestants were targets, as well as Greek Orthodox Christians living in Sicily and Southern Italy. At the time, these places were under Spanish rule.

The process of Inquisition began with a grace period that allowed anyone guilty of heresy to confess and repent. When the grace period was over, those running the Inquisition could make accusations. Defendants were interrogated and often tortured. Afterward, the accused were put on trial. It was extremely rare for anyone to be acquitted outright. More likely, the trial would be suspended. The person did not receive a guilty verdict, but he or she would remain under suspicion, and the Inquisition retained the right to resume the trial at any time. If found guilty, defendants could be "penanced," meaning they had to admit their heresy in public, after which they were sentenced for their crimes. The punishment could be anything from a fine to imprisonment in a dungeon or even torture. For extreme heresy, a defendant could be publicly executed. If the condemned repented, he or she was strangled and then set on fire. If the person did not repent, he or she was burned alive.

Although the number of trials decreased dramatically after the seventeenth century, the Inquisition was not abolished in Spain until July 1834. In all, around 5,000 people were executed during the Spanish Inquisition.

The Tribunal of the Inquisition
by Francisco de Goya

Leonardo's sketch of a large cannon being raised on to a gun-carriage. In later life, Leonardo moved away from painting and devoted his energies to science, including inventions, such as this early incarnation of a military tank.

The Inventor

From the beginning of his professional career, Leonardo divided his time between art and other interests, such as designing inventions. Though ingenious and based on science, few of his inventions were practical, especially considering the technology and materials then available. But the drawings reveal his innate genius for math and engineering, as well as his creative imagination in applying known principals to new ideas. Some of his drawings presage later innovations, such as bicycles and the helicopter.

During the mid-fifteenth century in Italy, several city-states, such as Florence and Pisa, were at war with one another. Military engineers were improving and developing firearms at an accelerated pace. Likewise, Leonardo had plenty of his own ideas for weaponry, which he sketched in his notebooks. He drew hand arms, projectiles, flamethrowers, crossbows, and other weapons. When he first wrote to Ludovico Sforza, Duke of Milan, he pitched himself not just as an artist but as an inventor, weapons designer, and civil engineer. His letter reads:

> Most illustrious Lord, having now sufficiently seen . . . all those who count themselves masters and inventors of instruments of war . . . I am emboldened without prejudice to anyone else to put myself in communication with your Excellency, in order to acquaint you with my secrets. . . .

I have plans for bridges, very light and strong and suitable for carrying very easily . . . and plans for burning and destroying those of the enemy.[1]

Leonardo told the duke he also knew how to construct battering rams, scaling ladders, cannons, and other tools that could break through an enemy fortress. After boasting that for sea warfare he could build a ship that could resist enemy bombardment, Leonardo describes what sounds like a crude tank: "Also I can make armored cars, safe and unassailable, which will enter the serried [crowded] ranks of the enemy with

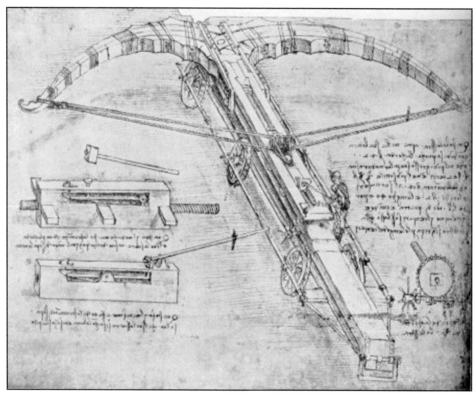

Leonardo's sketch of a giant crossbow on wheels. Leonardo offered his services to the duke of Milan. He was interested in designing weapons so that the city could defend itself from other Italian cities such as Pisa. Many of Leonardo's designs have been built and proven workable.

their artillery, and there is no company of men at arms so great that they will break it. And behind these the infantry will be able to follow quite unharmed and without any opposition."[2]

Turning his attention to peacetime, Leonardo pitched his services as an architect, canal designer, and, almost as an afterthought, an artist: "I can execute sculpture in marble, bronze, or clay, and also painting, in which my work will stand comparison with that of anyone else whoever he may be. . . . And if any of the aforesaid things should seem impossible or impractical to anyone, I offer myself as ready to make trial of them in . . . whatever place shall please your Excellency."[3]

For all of Leonardo's detailed plans and blueprints, documentarian Michael Mosely says his inventions remained largely hypothetical. "He's employed by warlords, but what they actually want him to do is to do things like make maps, paint portraits of their mistresses and mainly to organize their parties," Mosely explains. "He was a great party giver, one of the greatest of his age. . . . So there's no great evidence that any of the wonderful machines he designed he actually built."[4]

That did not deter Leonardo from sketching more designs. While working for the Vatican, he proposed heating water by using large concave mirrors to reflect sunlight onto the water—an example of solar power. In 1502, he was working on a civil engineering project for Istanbul's Sultan Beyazid II. He made a drawing of a single-span bridge that was 720 feet long—an unthinkable distance for a bridge at that time, but that was the distance across the waterway known as the Golden Horn. Beyazid thought it would be impossible to build such a long structure, but in 2001, an engineer in Norway constructed a small bridge based on Leonardo's design.

Similarly, a British skydiver risked life and limb to prove Leonardo's parachute design was viable. According to the *Guardian* newspaper, Adrian Nicholas "fulfilled his life's ambition to prove the aerodynamics experts wrong when he used a parachute based on Da Vinci's design to float almost one and a half miles down from a hot air balloon. Ignoring warnings that it would never work he built the 187 [pound] contraption of

Leonardo's *Two Designs for a Domed Church with Surrounding Cupolas.* What made his structural drawings intriguing is that he was just as interested in function as he was form. More than just design what a building or bridge would look like externally, his vision also included stairways, windows, and other elements.

wooden poles, canvas and ropes from a simple sketch that Da Vinci had scribbled in a notebook in 1485."[5]

Despite Leonardo's reputation as a gifted inventor and engineer, author Emil Ludwig says academics looked down upon the artist because he was not formally educated. "He felt scorn, most often a gentle scorn, for all sophists and philosophers."[6] Instead of learning by reading books written by the ancient Greeks and Romans, Leonardo learned by observing and investigating nature.

In 1490, Leonardo was walking through the country near Milan when he saw a ten-year-old boy drawing the goats he was tending. Leonardo was so smitten by the child that he offered to take care of the boy. The boy's father, who was poor and saw it as an opportunity for his son, agreed. Gian Giacomo Caprotti da Oreno was blond, curly haired, beautiful, and a hellion. His nickname was il Salaino, or Salai, which means "little devil" in Italian. Salai was characterized by Leonardo as a glutton, a thief, a liar, and overly stubborn. He repeatedly stole money and valuables from Leonardo so that he could go clothes shopping. At one point, he had accumulated 24 pairs of shoes. Although Salai exhibited some artistic talent, he wasn't good enough to make a living at it and continued to pilfer from Leonardo. Even so, Salai remained Leonardo's assistant and companion for nearly thirty years. Whether their relationship was ever romantic in nature can only be speculated.

Four sketches from Leonardo's notebooks. Leonardo had an uncanny ability to observe nature and accurately record it through his sketches and observations. He performed many autopsies in order to better understand the working of the human body.

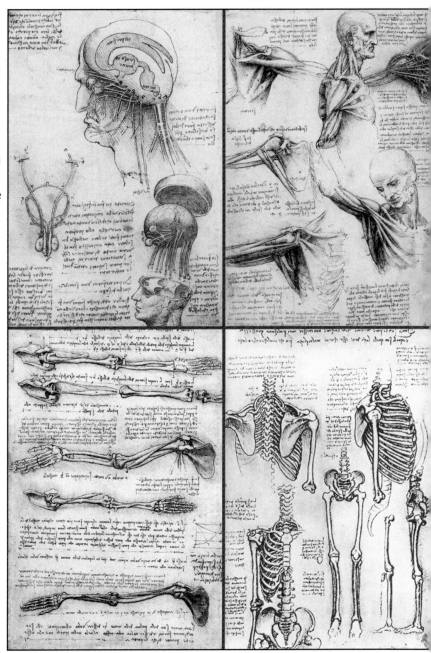

In April 2008 a Swiss daredevil named Olivier Vietti-Teppa built a parachute following Leonardo's design. Although he was unable to steer it, he safely floated to the ground. While Adrian Nicholas was the first to try Leonardo's parachute design, Vietti-Teppa was the first to use it without relying on a backup chute.

The same is true of Leonardo's relationship with Count Francesco Melzi. In 1506, the artist took on the fifteen-year-old Melzi as a student, but Francesco soon became his life companion and would be with Leonardo for the rest of the artist's life.

Salai and Melzi were the closest relationships of Leonardo's life. It seems that Leonardo could have been speaking about relationships in this passage from one of his notebooks: "Supreme happiness will be the greatest cause of misery . . ."[7]

While Leonardo kept his personal passions a closely guarded secret, his ardor for science would prove a gift he could share with the world.

Horse Sculpture, Leonardo da Vinci

Inventions

Although he is best known as an artist, Leonardo was a prolific inventor. He designed hundreds of machines and tools on paper but rarely followed through to build prototypes, or models. Some of his inventions were improvements on machines already in use, but many others were simply born from his imagination and knowledge of science. Here are some of his more intriguing, but lesser known, inventions:

Jack: In the days before cranes, lifting heavy objects during construction was a major engineering problem. Leonardo designed several devices using different forms of leverage—the pulley, the screw, and the ratchet—that are similar to modern jacks.

Printing Press: Gutenberg developed the printing press around 1440, but a half century later Leonardo improved the original design. His design used a lever to combine functions so that the press could be operated by one man instead of a team of printers. It would be almost 200 years before his improvements were applied.

Scaling Ladder: Many of Leonardo's inventions had military applications, such as his scaling ladder, which was raised and lowered by a crank attached to an oversized gear. With such a machine, soldiers could easily scale an enemy's fortress walls. Leonardo's design is similar to the ladders used by modern firemen.

Clock: Consistent accuracy in clocks was not achieved until the seventeenth century, when pendulums started being used as the regulating device. Two centuries earlier, Leonardo had depicted just such a device in a drawing.

Military Tank: Looking like a turtle, Leonardo's tank was propelled by men inside its shell who turned the wheels with cranks. In his notes he mused that such a machine would take the place of elephants and would frighten the enemy's horses.

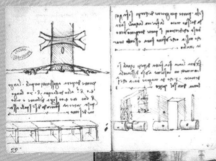

After seeing a model of Leonardo's pressed-bow bridge at an exhibition in 1996, Norwegian artist Vebjorn Sand was inspired to see the bridge become a reality. On October 31, 2001, the Norwegian Leonardo Bridge was opened to foot and bicycle traffic, marking the first time one of Leonardo's civil engineering designs was built for modern public use.

St. John the Baptist was Leonardo's final painting, created while he was living in Rome. Art historians believe the animal pelt St. John is wearing and the cross were added later by another artist.

The Scientist

It was Leonardo's attention to detail that made him such an accomplished scientist and inventor—and such an innovative artist. Although few people would think of science as art, or art as a kind of science, Leonardo uniquely blended the two in his quest to learn about the world around him.

His formal training in human anatomy started when he began studying under Verrocchio, who insisted that all his pupils learn anatomy. In learning how to paint and sculpt the human body, Leonardo drew many studies of the external aspects of bodies, such as shape and musculature.

But Leonardo wanted to know the body from the outside in. Once he became a successful artist, he was able to get permission from hospitals in Florence, Milan, and Rome to dissect corpses. He created at least two hundred meticulous drawings of the skeletal structure, circulatory system, reproductive system, and internal organs. He made one of the first scientific drawings of a fetus in utero. He studied how emotions such as anger affect physiology, or body functions. He was equally interested in animals, dissecting frogs, birds, cows, monkeys, and bears, and compared the animals' anatomy with that of humans. Leonardo recorded all his observations and drawings in notebooks that were mostly written in mirror writing.

Leonardo's curiosity knew few boundaries. Author Emil Ludwig noted Leonardo "was the first man since Archimedes to record the principles of the lever. In drawings which he made for the study of difficult problems in physics, he developed the law of the conservation of energy. When

wandering over the Maritime Alps he discovered mussels on the moun-taintops and founded the science of paleontology—then, he added what he knew of stratified rock, of fossils, and of tidal movements, all of which brought him back to astrological studies of an earlier period."[1]

In 1500, Leonardo returned to Florence. While there he allegedly had a confrontation with Michelangelo, who made fun of Leonardo for not having finished the equestrian statue. The mocking hurt Leonardo's feel-ings, and a feud began between the two celebrated artists.

In 1506, Leonardo went back to Milan at the request of its French gov-ernor, Charles d'Amboise. The king of France, Louis XII, was also living in Milan, and in 1507 Leonardo was named the king's court painter. For the next six years, Leonardo divided his time between Milan and Florence. In 1513 he moved to Rome to work for Giuliano de' Medici, a well-known patron of the arts. Leonardo stayed at the Vatican's Belvedere Palace. He established a workshop and spent most of the next two years studying anatomy and physiology. However, he felt intellectually restricted because the pope forbade him to dissect cadavers.

While in Rome, his health started to fade, and Leonardo was fre-quently ill. When he worked it was primarily on his science experiments. The only known painting from that period is the controversial *St. John the Baptist.* Many critics are uncomfortable with the way Leonardo portrays the saint as looking very feminine, with a smile reminiscent of Mona Lisa's. The blond mane of curls Leonardo gives John has made some suggest that the work is actually a representation of Salai.

Although he later created a number of new art oils and varnishes, it is believed that Leonardo essentially retired from painting after he left Rome in 1516 and moved to France. There, Francis I appointed him the Premier Painter and Engineer and Architect of the King. A very generous patron, Francis I gave Leonardo a salary and a manor house to use near the mon-arch's summer château at Amboise.

A stroke had left his right hand partially paralyzed, but being left-handed allowed Leonardo to continue teaching and drawing. Most of his time was spent organizing his notebooks. King Francis did not make

Leonardo's *Mona Lisa* hangs in the Louvre in Paris, France. It is estimated that over 5 million people a year view the *Mona Lisa*, widely considered to be the most famous painting in the world.

Leonardo fulfill any commissions, although he did have him produce plans for festivals and plays. While age might have hobbled his body, his intellect was as keen as ever—he built the king a mechanical lion with a chest that opened to reveal flowers.

Both Melzi and Salai traveled with Leonardo to France, but Salai returned to Milan in 1518 and built a house on the land Leonardo had inherited. Melzi stayed and was with Leonardo when he died on May 2, 1519, just a few weeks after his sixty-seventh birthday. Contrary to lore, Leonardo did not die being cradled by Francis I; the king was away celebrating the birth of his second son.

Leonardo was buried in the Church of St. Florentine, but his tomb was destroyed during the Wars of Religion. His remains were scattered and lost. Leonardo split his few possessions between his two companions. Melzi was given possession of Leonardo's notes; in all, Leonardo had filled about thirty notebooks, or codices, comprised of over 13,000 pages of writing, drawings, observations, and personal philosophy. The notebooks covered four main themes: architecture, elements of mechanics, painting, and human anatomy. After his death, some notes were lost, and his friends distributed the rest. Many of them were eventually collected by museums such as the Louvre and national libraries in Britain, Spain, and Italy. Only the Codex Leicester is privately owned.

The three paintings still among Leonardo's possessions—the *Mona Lisa*, the *Virgin and Child with St. Anne,* and *St. John the Baptist*—were bequeathed to Salai, who died in 1525 after a duel. (Some sources say he was murdered.)

Leonardo had never published his notebooks. Between that and the difficulty of reading his writing, it wasn't until the nineteenth century that his work became widely known. Once his notes were deciphered, the magnitude of his work was finally fully appreciated.

"Leonardo is the one artist of whom it may be said with perfect literalness: Nothing that he touched but turned into a thing of eternal beauty," wrote art historian Bernard Berenson. "Whether it be the cross section of a skull, the structure of a weed, or a study of muscles, he, with

Death of Leonardo da Vinci, painted by Jean-Auguste-Dominique Ingres. Although Leonardo died almost penniless, he left a rich, unprecedented legacy as an artist, inventor, and scientist.

his feeling for line and for light and shade, forever transmuted it into life-communicating values."[2]

French critic Hippolyte Taine was more effusive. "There may not be in the world an example of another genius so universal, so incapable of fulfillment, so full of yearning for the infinite, so naturally refined, so far ahead of his own century and the following centuries."[3]

The breadth of his achievements made Leonardo more than just an important historical figure; it made him the ultimate Renaissance man, who continues to inspire both artists and scientists the world over.

The Codex Leicester

Throughout his life Leonardo kept notebooks of his scientific writings and illustrations. The notebooks are in Leonardo's unique mirror writing and are filled with illustrations. He believed that too much text confused the reader while illustrations made it easier to understand concepts. It is believed 31 remain in existence. His Codex Leicester is the most famous of all his notebooks and was compiled between 1506 and 1510 while Leonardo was in Milan. The Codex, or volume, was named after Thomas Cook, the first Earl of Leicester, who bought it in 1717. The codex is made up of eighteen sheets of paper, written on both sides and folded in half, resulting in a 72-page document. No longer bound, the sheets are now displayed separately.

Taken together, his notebooks deal with four main themes: painting, architecture, mechanics, and human anatomy. The Codex Leicester contains Leonardo's observations and theories on astronomy and geology, including his theory on why fossils are found on mountains: Leonardo believed that mountains had originally been seabeds that gradually rose out of the water until they became mountains. He also speculated that the slight glow on the dark portion of the crescent moon was caused by light reflected from the earth. One hundred years later, German astronomer Johannes Kepler proved the phenomenon of "planetshine." The main topic of the Codex is the movement of water, or hydraulics, and how it responds to different conditions.

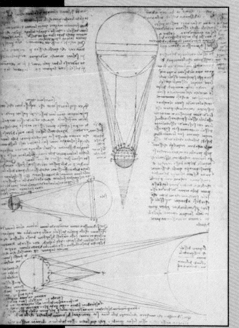

A page from the Codex Leicester

Since Cook bought the Codex, it has remained privately owned. In 1980, industrialist Armand Hammer, an avid art collector, purchased the document from the Leicester estate and renamed it the Codex Hammer. Microsoft founder Bill Gates bought the notebook at an auction for $30.8 million, making it the most expensive book ever. He changed its name back to Codex Leicester and now puts it on display once a year, picking a different host city every year.

To preserve Leonardo's work, Gates had the Codex's pages scanned into digital image files. When Windows Vista was released in England in January 2007, Gates and the British Library, which owns Leonardo's Codex Arundel, put the two notebooks online for six months for the public to view. It was the first time in 500 years the notebooks could be viewed side by side.

CHRONOLOGY

1452	Leonardo is born in Anchiano on April 15
1468	Leonardo's grandfather dies at the age of ninety-six
1469	Leonardo starts apprenticeship with Andrea del Verrocchio in Florence
1472	He is accepted into Company of Painters
1475	Begins work on *The Annunciation*
1478	Becomes an independent master; completes *Madonna and the Child*
1480	Designs the first workable parachute
1482	Moves to Milan
1483	Begins work on *The Virgin of the Rocks*
1487	Starts his anatomy studies
1499	Flees Milan after France invades Italy
1500	Visits Venice and Florence
1502	Hired by Cesare Borgia as military engineer
1503	Begins *Mona Lisa*
1506	Invited to Milan by French governor Charles d'Amboise
1507	Returns to Florence and named court painter to Louis XII
1508	Returns to Milan; completes *The Virgin of the Rocks*
1513	Hired by Giuliano de' Medici in Rome
1514	Receives patronage of new pope, Leo X
1516	Moves to France; works for Francis I
1519	Dies at the Castle of Cloux near Amboise, France, on May 2

TIMELINE IN HISTORY

1378	Pope Gregory XI dies.
1400	Author and poet Geoffrey Chaucer dies.
1423	The earliest known woodcut is issued.
1431	Joan of Arc is burned at the stake.
1436	Johannes Gutenberg builds the first printing press.
1445	An outbreak of the Black Plague hits London.
1451	Concave lenses for eyeglasses are invented.
1453	The fall of Constantinople ends the Byzantine Empire.
1460	The first book on surgery is published.
1473	Michelangelo paints the ceiling of the Sistine Chapel.
1483	Raphael is born at Urbino.
1492	Columbus lands in the New World.
1497	Vasco de Gama sails around the Cape of Good Hope.
1515	Nicolaus Copernicus theorizes that planets move around the sun.
1545	Council of Trent convenes to clarify Catholic Church doctrine.
1579	The first glass eyes are manufactured.

Paintings

Annunciation (1475–1480)
Ginevra de' Benci (c. 1475)
The Benois Madonna (1478–1480)
The Virgin with Flowers (1478–1481)
Adoration of the Magi (1481)
Cecilia Gallerani with an Ermine
  (1488–1490)
A Musician (c. 1490)
Madonna Litta (1490–1491)
La Belle Ferronière (1495–1498)
The Last Supper (1498)
The Madonna of the Rocks (1483–
  1486)
Mona Lisa (*La Gioconda*) (1503–1506)
Battle of Anghiari (Lost painting)
  (1505)
The Virgin of the Rocks (1508)
Leda and the Swan (1508)
The Virgin and Child with St. Anne
  (c. 1510)
St. John the Baptist (c. 1510)
Bacchus (1515)

Inventions

Armored car
Hang glider
Scissors
Life preserver
Double-hulled boat
Water-driven saw
Diving equipment
Catapult
Movable bridge
Wall-scaling systems
Robot
Machine gun
Submarine
Parachute
Helicopter

LEONARDO DA VINCI

CHAPTER NOTES

Chapter 1. Legal Woes

1. Kenneth Clark, *Leonardo da Vinci: An Account of His Development as an Artist* (New York: Macmillan, 1939), p. 143.

2. Ibid., p. 48.

Chapter 2. Prodigy

1. NPR, Talk of the Nation, "Analysis: Leonardo da Vinci's Life and Work," January 16, 2003, http://www.highbeam.com/doc/IP1-71079463.html

2. Leonardo da Vinci, *The Notebooks of Leonardo da Vinci*, translated by Irma Anne Richter (Cambridge: Oxford University Press, 1998), p. 286.

Chapter 3. The Artist

1. Miranda Seymour, "Father of Invention," *The Sunday [London] Times Culture*, January 9, 2000, pp. 35–36.

2. Bruce Johnson. "Does This Picture Hide a Lost Leonardo?" *The Daily Telegraph*, July 17, 2000, p. 3.

Chapter 4. The Inventor

1. Leonardo da Vinci, *The Notebooks of Leonardo da Vinci*, http://www.fullbooks.com/The-Notebooks-of-Leonardo-Da-Vinci-Complete15.html

2. Ibid.

3. Ibid.

4. NPR, Talk of the Nation, "Analysis: Leonardo da Vinci's Life and Work," January 16, 2003. http://www.highbeam.com/doc/IP1-71079463.html

5. Julia Hartley-Brewer, "Skydiver Proves Da Vinci Chute Works." *The Guardian*, June 28, 2000, p. 9.

6. Emil Ludwig, *Genius and Character*, translated by Kenneth Burke (New York: Harcourt, Brace and Company, 1927), p. 154.

7. Leonardo da Vinci, *The Notebooks of Leonardo da Vinci*, http://www.fullbooks.com/The-Notebooks-of-Leonardo-Da-Vinci-Completex5324.html

Chapter 5. The Scientist

1. Emil Ludwig, *Genius and Character*, translated by Kenneth Burke (New York: Harcourt, Brace and Company, 1927), p. 154.

2. Bernard Berenson. *The Florentine Painters of the Renaissance* (New York: G.P. Putnam's Sons, 1909), p. 67.

3. The Global Art, *Leonardo da Vinci*, from Hippolyte Taine's *Philosophy of Art in Italy*, http://www.theglobalart.com/Leonard_da_vinci.html

FURTHER READING

Books

Anderson, Maxine. *Amazing Leonardo da Vinci Inventions You Can Build Yourself.* White River Junction, Vermont: Nomad Press, 2006.

Edwards, Roberta, True Kelley (Illustrator). *Who Was Leonardo da Vinci?* New York: Grosset & Dunlap, 2005.

Hodge, Susie. *The Life of Leonardo Da Vinci.* Grand Rapids, Michigan: School Specialty Publishing, 2006.

Langley, Andrew. *The Da Vinci Kit: Mysteries of the Renaissance Decoded.* Philadelphia: Running Press Book Publishers, 2006.

Romei, Francesca, Sergio Ricciardi, Andrea Ricciardi. *Leonardo da Vinci : Artist, Inventor and Scientist of the Renaissance.* New York: Peter Bedrick Books, 2001.

Works Consulted

Clark, Kenneth. *Leonardo Da Vinci: An Account of His Development as an Artist.* New York: Macmillan, 1939.

Hartley-Brewer, Julia. "Skydiver Proves Da Vinci Chute Works." *The Guardian,* June 28, 2000. pg 9.

Kausal, Martin. *Leonardo da Vinci.* 2004. http://www.kausal.com.

Ludwig, Emil. *Genius and Character.* Translated by Kenneth Burke. New York: Harcourt, Brace and Company, 1927.

Nuland, Sherwin B. *Leonardo da Vinci.* New York: Lipper Viking Books, 2000.

Seymour, Miranda. "Father of Invention." *The Sunday [London] Times Culture.* January 9, 2000.

Stanley, Diane. *Leonardo da Vinci.* New York: Morrow Books, 1996.

Turner, Richard A. *Inventing Leonardo.* University of California Press, 1994.

Vasari, Giorgio. *The Lives of the Artists.* Translated by Julia Conaway Bondanella and Peter Bondanella. Oxford : Oxford University Press, 1998.

Zollner Frank, and Johannes Nathan. *Leonardo da Vinci: The Complete Paintings and Drawings.* London: Taschen, 2003.

On the Internet

BBC. "Mona Lisa Smile Secrets Revealed." February 18, 2003
news.bbc.co.uk/1/hi/entertainment/arts/2775817.stm

Leonardo da Vinci: A Genius Before His Time
http://www.unmuseum.org/leonardo.htm

Leonardo da Vinci, *The Notebooks of Leonardo da Vinci*
http://www.fullbooks.com/The-Notebooks-of-Leonardo-Da-Vinci-Completex5324.html

Museum of Science, *Leonardo da Vinci: Scientist, Inventor, Artist*
http://www.mos.org/leonardo/

NPR, Talk of the Nation, "Analysis: Leonardo da Vinci's Life and Work," January 16, 2003. http://www.highbeam.com/doc/IPI-71079463.html

PBS Treasures of the World: Mona Lisa
http://www.pbs.org/treasuresoftheworld/a_nav/mona_nav/main_monafrm.html

S. C. Williams Library: Da Vinci's Inventions
www.lib.stevens-tech.edu/collections/davinci.html

The Institute and Museum of the History of Science, *The Mind of Leonardo*
brunelleschi.imss.fi.it/menteleonardo

Virtual Leonardo da Vinci Museum
www.leonet.it/comuni/vinci

GLOSSARY

anatomy (ah-NAA-tuh-mee)—The study of the structure of animals; the study of body parts.

apocryphal (ah-PAH-kruh-ful)—Of doubtful origins; not able to be verified.

chiaroscuro (kee-ar-uh-SKYOOR-oh)—The use of light and dark to create an illusion of depth; a term in art for a contrast between light and dark.

commission (kuh-MIH-shun)—To hire for a fee or salary; the fee or salary received for a particular job.

dogma (DOG-muh)—A religious belief.

fresco (FRESS-koh)—A type of painting done on wet plaster using watercolors.

hypothetical (hy-poh-THEH-tih-kul)—Existing in thought only.

illegitimate (il-eh-JIH-tih-mit)—Having parents who are not married according to the laws of the church.

paleontology (pay-lee-on-TAH-luh-jee)—The study of life in the past based on fossil evidence.

prototype (PROH-toh-typ)—Model; first of a kind.

prowess (PROW-ess)—Superior skill or ability.

monastery (MAH-nuh-stayr-ee)—The residence of monks.

sfumato (sfoo-MAH-toh)—A painting technique that overlays translucent layers of color to create perceptions of depth, volume, and form; the blending of colors or tones to obscure outlines or boundaries.

sophist (SAH-fist)—A philosopher.

stigma (STIG-muh)—Disgrace; social disapproval.

INDEX